FAREWELL MY LOVELY

Polly Clark was born in Toronto in 1968 and brought up in Lancashire, Cumbria and the Borders of Scotland. She has worked variously as a zookeeper, a teacher of English in Hungary and in publishing at Oxford University Press. In 1997 she won an Eric Gregory Award for her poetry.

Her first collection, *Kiss* (Bloodaxe Books, 2000), was a Poetry Book Society Recommendation. Her second, *Take Me With You* (Bloodaxe Books, 2005), a Poetry Book Society Choice, was shortlisted for the T.S. Eliot Prize. *Farewell My Lovely* (Bloodaxe Books, 2009) is her third collection. She has also published short stories. Polly now lives on the West Coast of Scotland and is a Royal Literary Fund Fellow at Edinburgh University. She can be found on the internet at www.pollyclark.co.uk.

POLLY CLARK

Farewell
My Lovely

BLOODAXE BOOKS

ISBN: 978 1 85224 825 3

First published 2009 by
Bloodaxe Books Ltd,
Highgreen,
Tarset,
Northumberland NE48 1RP.

www.bloodaxebooks.com
For further information about Bloodaxe titles
please visit our website or write to
the above address for a catalogue.

Bloodaxe Books Ltd acknowledges
the financial assistance of
Arts Council England, North East.

Cover design: Neil Astley & Pamela Robertson-Pearce.

Cover printing: J. Thomson Colour Printers Ltd, Glasgow.

Printed in Great Britain by
Bell & Bain Limited, Glasgow, Scotland.

For Julian

ACKNOWLEDGEMENTS

Acknowledgements are due to the editors of the following publications in which some of these poems first appeared: *London Review of Books*, *Poetry London*, *Poetry Review* and *Pratik*. 'Advice to a Daughter' was written for Keiren Phelan for his birthday.

I am very grateful to the Scottish Arts Council for a Writing Bursary in 2006 which gave me time to write, and to Gavin Wallace for his confidence in me.

Acknowledgements are due to the soldiers and officers of the Falklands War whose accounts of the conflict inspired *I Thought It Was in Scotland*.

For his generous criticism and care I am grateful to Matthew Hollis. Thanks are due also to Joanne Limburg, Antony Dunn, Clare Pollard and the students of the Fielding Programme who read and gave helpful comments on some of these poems. A special thank you is due to Jan Clyde, whose kindness knows no bounds.

CONTENTS

I Thought It Was in Scotland:
A FALKLANDS MEMOIR

Bay Tree

I longed for a home.
God gave me someone else's.

I longed to escape my past.
God gave me someone else's.

I longed to be forgiven.
God said, *how can you be?*

For you know what you do.
Instead of forgiveness

God gave me a bay tree
that flickers with finches.

I think he means it
to be a lesson.

When the sun rises over my view
I don't know where I am.

I longed to love.
God gave me you.

You Would Drop Your Spade

There's a god in my head,
quiet, inventive, ambitious,

trying with the unfamiliar
scraps of what's available –

beaches, birches, bungalows,
rubbish, rhodies, retirees –

to recast the shell she occupies
so that you might look up

suddenly from the garden
and see exactly what you lost

coming back to you: a gift
for which faith is not necessary.

You would drop your spade
and cross the garden smiling,

slip your hands into the holes
of this resurrected thing,

kiss it, and know again
the perfect solace of its skin.

Tour of Landscapes by the Artist

My first:
a father waiting
in an empty tree.
Note his sulky wings,
his shabby stamp
on the sky's gauze.
What is he waiting for,
with no sorrow,
no blink or flap.

My second:
a watercolour teary
as an eye graze.
The sun bent the sky
and I could see lives
magnified from miles away.
All of them I pulled
dripping with light
from the chemical sea.

My latest
(in progress):
a sound piece.
The scowl of a speedboat
undoing the sea.
Note the husband
weeping
in the blaze of the trees.

Shoes

The husband gets home on time.
Each day he is happier, she sees it

like health overwhelming his tired frame,
sweeping away all things unhappy.

On the step she sees her husband's shoes
bent from the happy way he walks.

They point happily towards the house.
No love, no marriage, no fury

nor ecstasy have ever brought
anything of him to her door before.

She watches happily as the shoes
sit patiently in the long evening.

The husband is starting supper
happily in the kitchen.

The wife smiles all the happy evening,
while the shoes wait, warm as dogs.

Marriage

I got married and everything was different.
It seemed impolite to leave, so I didn't.

I began to observe the traces
of my husband, his neatly folded sweaters,

the spaces where he pressed
his life before me.

To touch pictures of him when he was young
made me afraid. I couldn't stop crying,

while my husband brought flowers
and said how sorry he was.

My clothes became too small, as if
they belonged to a sister or a child I'd never had.

Someone said, *you are blooming*.
Of course they could not know

the violence of my marriage.
It broke my heart like a nose.

Its strength shocked me.
Dragged me. Reset me.

Bar Harbor, Maine

Here is where we took the boat
across the harbour whose bed

crawls with lobsters clamouring
me please! me please!

who since babyhood
have been thrown back

until the day the familiar hand
closes round a fat blue waist,

and, waving in anticipation,
they land in adult surprise –

here is where we lay side by side
on the pink hotel bed.

Here is where the islands
rose out of the haze,

and you walked the shingle
tracked by a shadow

like a stray that has decided
the future is with you,

scrabbling to catch you,
asking no further questions.

Farewell My Lovely

A really good detective never gets married.
RAYMOND CHANDLER

I'd gotten used to that roomy grin,
the face like a bag of facts,
the flank round as a pony's,
and the way she had of blending in
so badly. But after all,
I didn't really know her,
neither she nor I being the intimate type.

      I take a slug of something
that I've been craving, make a note
of everything that's gone with her.
But my notes become a list
of immovables: this slouching house,
the sea with a face I'd like to smack,
the loosening sky, fit to drop –

      as I'm dusting the mirror
I glimpse her, smart as a rat
in the company of rocks –
but the day's slammed shut
and it's time to file the file.
This is a face to be turned over
for answers from now on.

She's left nothing behind her
to show what was between us.
Always meticulous,
      I find she's slipped
like a last dram into my dreams,
hunched at the scene, wiping fingerprints,
knowing that it's over, that it's time to go.

Friends

It showed how friendship
doesn't end (like when
Emma and I watched

eight episodes in one go)
though outside my window
the climate was changing

and in my experience
people found each other
quite easy to take or leave.

The day after the last episode
they ran them all again,
protecting me, it seems.

I keep just one from
two-hundred-and-thirty-six.
It's the one where Ross says,

but this can't be it,
and Rachel says,
then how come it is?

and he sinks to his knees with his arms
around her legs and the camera
moves slowly back

and they hold the shot
for a long time
before the theme tune begins.

Disorder

My hands are alcoholics
trembling with regret.

My feet are co-dependent,
plodding after the dead,

the frozen, the vanished.
My gut's an obsessive:

I've eaten the same meal
all my life, just like Kafka.

It's the only way I feel
safe, or optimistic at all.

My eyes are bi-polar,
seeing too much and not enough;

and of my sectioned ears
only a sliver is visible.

They're ashamed of the pain
that is their life now

and the rabble
they're stuck with

is, with the best will in the world,
fucking up their recovery.

Yariguies Brush Finch

British-led expedition discovers
new species of bird (October 2006).

You may be dead already,
nipped upright by giant hands,

or perhaps the loll of your head,
beak clamped shut and wings

slammed against escape
simply cry your bewilderment.

I've seen it before: the hunch of the body
when revelations are trawled from the dark,

the body pathetic in its plumage,
flapping a language no one understands.

But without this tiny violence
we will be poorer:

our possession of you
may teach us all we need to know.

Wake little bird. No secret
can resist these gentle hands.

Last Night I Dreamed of England

Last night I dreamed of England,
and I wept in the morning

for my love
of everything gentle.

I wept for the spires
and the meadows

that smiled on me for years
and let me live near them.

I wept for the surly
northern cities

that came, in the end,
to envy me.

Didn't you see me
dressed up as someone

who knows someone?
Didn't you see me

in the beds
of my betters?

Last night I dreamed of England
and I wept in the morning

for the gentle thing
I nearly became,

for the work of art
I was in England.

Drowning

Knowing they'd be gone
I could smile at his pink face,

his smart shirt and tie,
his desperation to go.

I could be amused
by her whisperings about Jesus

and how everything's for the children,
and how you can never complain

about the children.
Tonight I turned up Springsteen

to bursting volume to drown
the babies' screaming

the clattering up and down,
the stompings, the shoutings.

The air trembled as if an enormous heart
was growing beneath their floor,

swelling to terrible proportions,
pumping apocalypse into their walls,

and I waited for the promise
of a new life to come true,

for the morning to bring me
beautiful, empty wreckage.

Kilcreggan

Craggy scowl filled with water,
dream-gagger, home-wrecker.

Was there somewhere better here
before the mountains cracked their grin,

the wind grieved across the rocks
and winter battered marriage,

the shop twirled its sign to SHUT
and the formless sea howled

that those who shall inherit the earth
are the righteous and the grey.

Dog Opera

...tracking between
rigidity and delight,
never resolving,

so I thought of him as music,
but he was simply waiting
for the moment

that would reveal him,
and one afternoon
she emerged –

her speckled belly
set him moaning:
he fixed on her heels,

his body a god
unfolding in black.
His tongue begged

for a taste of her
as the trees parted,
the mud applauding,

calling them back
and back again
to reveal the finale:

a spotlit clearing,
a dog bowing,
flowers everywhere.

Little Black Dog

Take, for instance, the ferns:
one nudge from the sky
and they swirl with all the green
of their first September,

and take the little black dog,
bolting through the scree of sky,
bending and unbending himself
like a letter in determined hands –

he stops at the call of his name
and looks back – he believes the sound,
though the sea convulses
with a universe of names just like it.

The still-green leaves
lie where they were blown,
face down and completely still,
but take, for instance, dying:

the trees are insisting
God doesn't mean it, they insist –
billowing like fabulous ash –
that everything can begin again.

Our Baby

shows us that longing
is the matter from which

everything is made,
and when the morning

brims at the window
our baby is fearless.

She faces down
her non-existence,

she regards her would-
be parents kindly.

She watches us endure
the days and nights without her.

Our baby teaches us
to live tenaciously.

In these hard, shining days,
we come to know her.

Moon

It was lost, it did not belong
above this stripped hillside,

the yawn of the estuary,
the chatter of little houses.

It peeped over the hill's shoulder
like an infant, glowing

as the sick do when all else
has failed and God has arrived.

Unable to stop, it rose on,
vast, naked, unable to hide:

the one face we can't forget,
staring back at us from the road.

Trash

Down beside the sour low tide
where Mickey Mouse's yellow hand
drifts across his bursting heart,

the rocks lay out their washed-up wares:
the chins and ears of fancy cups
where grandmas pressed their lips,

the plate's edge I remember
from school, its blue rim
smart and plump as a teapot.

All the teatimes of my childhood
have been smashed here,
and when the tide recedes again

I'm back, pockets stupidly full,
hungry for a time before I knew
I'd be a scavenger of my life.

Laparoscopy

Doctor Corolla from Egypt
will pump me with CO_2,

then slip a camera through
a hole he'll create, and observe.

I will be fast asleep
when Doctor Corolla

ticks off my name,
parts the waves of my gown.

Slow, he explains later
when I cling to his cuff.

But I say six months
you will be pregnant.

Behind shrunken curtains
the women are weeping

as Doctor Corolla
moves from bed to bed.

Endometriosis late stage.
Chance of conceiving

now 30 percent.
This is what I am telling you.

A girl smiles thinly from her bed
and I am sick on the kerb.

The sea is nothing to me.
I have a scar, and a promise.

Bulletin

It's raining wolves.
The mud has crossed
the line into corruption.
A heron grabs the last flight out.
Reeds are creating
an illegal settlement on the lawn.
My wall is nearly up.
It cuts me in half
but life is more peaceful.
I refuse to answer
any of the night's whispers.
The world unites
in condemnation.
Someone is launching
everything they've got.
The sky is free-falling.
8.00 A.M. The pips.
Welcome to *Today*.

Return to Eden

When we were allowed back
we saw the place had changed.

Sea licked its borders,
fish flashed like knives.

Nothing pleased us. Nothing lived up
to what we had suffered to return.

But then, today –
the tiny ghost we see on the screen,

moving inside me without sorrow.
Is it not the shape of everything

before we lost it?
My darling, are we not forgiven?

Magnificat

Imagine. Your eyes open
onto an angel made of the sea.

Imagine the instruction:
God has chosen you to be

the vessel for his dream.
Instantly the suburbs

become a world of meaning.
The women gather round you,

desperate to touch you.
Imagine. The word *glory*

finally describes the sun
on your geraniums.

You pity your neighbours,
even as they trespass on your lawn.

The butcher stained with blood
is a force for good,

the corner shopkeeper
glows with kindness.

Imagine. You get in your car
and you drive and drive.

Imagine. Nothing in this world
can save you now.

Beheaded

I hear perfectly: the thud
onto linen, the strange gasp
like the cry of a premature baby,
just once and then silence.

And I see perfectly:
how my lashes scratch the light,
a hair glittering in shadow,
the winded hollow

where my lips rest.
I still have all my words.
I move my mouth,
like someone begging for water.

Fingers grab my hair
and I soar high above my sad
old body, slumped and tiny.
Tears of pity for it fill my eyes.

They are tending it,
the blank women in blue.
They are washing it,
as if they loved it.

Look, the people are cheering me,
look, they are glad to see me,
now that I've been removed
without a single word of protest.

She

(after Charles Aznavour)

She may be a shadow of the past
etched in my body, in my face,
the love that could not hope to last.

She may be the life that's passed,
the road that leaves the faintest trace,
she may be a shadow of the past.

And from her tiny hand is cast
the love that never found a place,
the love could not hope to last

and now is, like youth, surpassed
by her determined, warm embrace.
She may be a shadow of the past.

She may make the night sky vast
and her cries write in empty space
of love that could not hope to last.

In darkened rooms I hold her fast.
I hold her while the planets race.
She may be a shadow of the past,
the love that could not hope to last.

Special Care Unit

This is where the premature
meet the very old,

dissolving the world's edges
with their soft, accepting sucks.

Each day we cross fifty miles
of broken, birthed earth,

the road twisting into golden fog.
Mountains weep in corners,

are broad-chested and no-nonsense,
and tenderness kicks everywhere:

the practical faces of midwives,
the knife-cleanliness of alcohol,

my husband's hand that was never so strong
until it reached inside an incubator,

and this lonely road,
the canal between darkness and light.

Each night I see my daughter,
my mother, myself,

with tiny, gummy mouth
whispering, *My darling girl,*

who are you?
Have you come to take me home?

Ladies

arrive right on time
at your door in the rain

with special equipment
for mulching your brain.

They appear to be women,
they have fluffy names

but they have since undergone
some terrible change.

They growl misinformation
and coo in your phone

ring us soon Lucy's Mum
ring us soon soon soon.

Women, get a husband
who will say when they've gone

phew! I'd like a pint
of whatever she's on

and women, keep your husband!
Tend him well, like a border.

Don't let him leave you,
keep your home in good order

or you'll bring them sprinting
in grave disappointment

clipboards glinting
without an appointment.

Directions

To the left (depending which way
you come) you'll find

a ravenous sea (although
you haven't got the wrong place

if it's furious, or sashaying
in its blue off-the-shoulder).

You'll also see a bus shelter,
and the entrance to School Road.

Keep going. On the right,
a line of old villas, neatly rotting,

and twinkling now it's winter.
Wrapped-up shapes wander in and out

some with children,
some with dogs.

If you come to the Burgh Hall
you've gone too far – turn back

before the rain and wind
make any return impossible.

You've found the house when you see
white gates which will be shut.

A wrapped-up shape
wanders in and out,

sometimes with a baby
sometimes with a dog.

The First Woman

I became the woman
running out in her slippers

to touch the destroyer
resting at the gate;

I became the woman
who carried her baby

from window to window
like a flare.

I became the woman
weeping on the hour,

who watched *Big Brother*
as minesweepers

gathered on the lawn.
I became the first woman

militarily proven
to disappear.

Smile

Sometimes
I forget her

(she's very small
she doesn't speak)

and all that happens
is that she wakes

without me
and she smiles

or cries a little
without me.

It fills my head
on the train

or in my hotel bed
the smile

that comes and goes
without me.

Bitch

Scrawny, faded, money-
grubbing, gold-digging hags.
Hard-nosed, know-what-they-
want-manipulators, got-him-

right-where-they-want-him,
who-does-she-think-she-is
witches. Got her nails into him,
and he doesn't even see it:

my father's smug succession
of women who will not cry
at his beside, nor love his children,
nor think of his terrible lies.

How I hate them, as I slip alone
into my white dress. My father is long-
gone, everything jostles to fill the space.
When I enter the church I hear them,

I see them in the unsmiling faces
of your old friends who turn to look.
Who-does-she-think-she-is, no-mark-
from-nowhere, she's going to break

your poor old heart, she's going to take
everything you've got, cold bitch
who doesn't even know you, what would
your mother say, why are you smiling.

Islay

Thirty years ago, I'm sure you lifted
your eyes from her shore, and your gaze
drifted to this rock on the mainland
where I stand remembering you –

as today at the marina, when my husband
glimpsed the *Innisfree*, a boat he knew
long ago. Someone had made her new,
polished the years from her gleaming bow.

He fell silent as she pulled out to sea.
Just like that I think you'd know me now
as if the ocean, the islands, the sun between,
and all we love more had never been.

Another Girl

For I have got
another girl –

another girl –
who will love me till the end.

I don't want to say
I've been unhappy with you

but I have got another girl
who never really went away,

who wakes each day
saying my name,

whose happiness
I promised I would find.

You're making me say
I've got nobody but you

but every promise I made you
I made another girl

and in every dream of you
is another girl.

I don't want to say
I haven't loved you,

'cos it wouldn't be true,
it's just that I have got (*to fade*)

The Book of Truths

Under the spreading tree
she pounds the grass,

gives me a long clear
look like a stream

running into the sea.
She squints at the clouds

and smiles; she believes
in them, and in me.

Silently I read to my baby.
Part The First:

Things to Believe
All Your Life –

The earth will not die
and leave you alone.

When the seas overflow,
you will be saved.

Santa, and God,
will watch over you.

I will never disappoint you.
Part the Last:

Don't Read This
Until the Rest no Longer Holds.

Some people, my darling,
some people are just cunts.

Baby Group

Save me from my loneliness,
lady of the scar,

lady of the birth trauma
and the absent husband.

Distract me in the rain,
lady of the Asda fairy cake,

vacantly sipping as angels
circle in babywalkers.

And you, lady of perfection,
Boudica of cashmere

whose baby's shoes are shiny,
whose ribbons reek of adoration,

though we may never say more
than *hello, isn't she lovely!*

I am glad you exist.
You appear on a grey morning

right on time, smart as a sail
on bewildered waters.

Last Will and Testament

To Hamish the dog: my blankets, my best rattle, the blocks he chewed.
To my mother: my mattress where my head has made a dip,
                 all the photographs.
To my father: his spectacles, which he let me take from his nose and break,
                 also my lacy shoes and all my frozen spinach.
To Auntie Jan: the pink cardigan she made me, also my butterfly.
To my mother in addition: my washable nappies (for re-sale), Gina Ford,
                 my weaning spoons.
To my father in addition: my words (my *da-da*, my *ba-ba*), my mother,
                 my best red trousers.

Struck

What made the air ball its fist
and hurl me down?

I didn't curse, simply my wife
surfaced on the crest of pain,

gasping – or was it me
opening and closing my mouth?

I will always remember –
she tried to carry me, and could not.

She pressed her palms to the earth
pronounced it freezing and a terrible distance.

She frowned at the mathematical problem of me
as I dragged my leg like a giant parenthesis.

The air, blowing its knuckles, retreated,
as my wife held me, angel of gas-and-air.

* *

In hospital a woman
inhabited me.

She sat amongst my broken bones
and admonished me.

She was always charming
to busy, evil nurses.

She, too, was undressed for the journey
to the windowless basement

where men in green with speedy names
lean over in masks and exeunt.

Even she at the final second
pointed frantically at medical papers,

and stammered a hope, a wish,
for this or that kindness,

until she was coshed
with technical correctness,

and woke up lashing out
and would not *stop shouting Mr Forrester!*

She moaned in the tunnel of striplights.
She gathered ease, time, cleanliness,

and packed them grimly
like a disappointed wife.

She shut up only when the morphine arrived.
But I knew her, just the same.

    *   *

And though I broke it off cleanly
when my wife arrived with flowers

so that she never knew a thing
and she received me home in sunlight,

the memory came home with me
and occupied the night's bright hours.

In the sunny winter where leaves
drift over the lawn and into the sea,

my wife and I hold hands like newly-weds.
We kiss. We watch films all day.

Our baby squeals at her reflection
which copies her exactly, and soundlessly.

Soup

makes me cry.
I find it on my doorstep

with an initial of twigs
on its lid, or in the arms

of a woman who knows
how emptiness lives.

Lentil, chicken, beef.
Freeze it, they say.

Sorry it's not much.
I made it today.

Blessed are the soup-
makers. Blessed

are their feet
that bring them to my door.

Blessed are their hands,
blessed are their eyes

that brim quietly
with all they know.

Chair-o-plane

Mini-funfair. Princes Street.
My taxi pulls out of Waverley station,

hovers on the brink of the road,
then grinds up the Mound –

and that's when he catches me,
the man in black in the chair-o-plane,

arms gaping, wrists like stars.
He knocks my breath out

from a quarter-of-a-mile.
He's like a suit with the body

blown out. He shocks me
with his tiny, rigid offer

high above the buses.
He commands me,

make a poem of me,
me, here, on the funfair ride,

me, here, the man in black.
Man in the chair-o-plane,

you terrify me.
Silently you cry to be lifted,

as if you were mine,
out of the dazzling day.

A Bench for Me

To help me sleep
I used to imagine dancing here.

Stupid, I know. After all
it's a hillside above a city.

Highland cows glower
over the fence. Guanacos

dip and flutter beyond.
And everything is tiny

and further away
than you thought.

Here is where I learned
the only lesson that stuck:

that the body is for others
but the face is yours

to press to the breathing side
of something fiercely alive –

the muntjak perhaps
with its flickering skin,

or the macaw, whose feathers
are warm as lips,

covering your eyes softly
as if you were a child.

Sex in the City

Look at that road
sliced open like a cake,
a cake for me,
surrounded by men
in mucky yellow
their heads thrown back.
I can't take my eyes
off the layers:
the black frosting of tarmac,
its steaming bitumen sauce
then the drool of gravel,
the crunch of hardcore,
and at the very bottom
the men standing knee deep
in a sludge of iron
and laughing, laughing
as if their lovers
had surprised them.

Thank You

It was the kind of light
that rocks bend to drink,
and the man in the cowboy hat
with the swans at his feet
braced himself against the gleam.
All the sadness of the hills
was on fire. The swan-galleons
set sail across the grey.
And I ran the length of the loch
to press into your hand this –
for the shining silver of my life.

Advice to a Daughter

One day you will need help
I cannot give. Certain things

to do with your soul,
which of course is yours alone.

My only advice: one day
someone will cross your path

who spots you're special,
is so convinced in fact

that you become so.
You will probably forget

to thank them, so quietly
did they change your life.

All I can say, darling,
is watch out –

not for the hurts,
they will come and go.

But for those who properly see you.
So that when your life

has turned as it should
you will know to whom it's due.

To My Husband

This face, this book, this daughter
I commend to you, unfinished.
Read them, darling, and know me.
Keep the rules and the routines:
they will free your nights for dreams,
and in keeping them, you know me.
Stay here, in this old house.
Keep my books on a good shelf
away from the sun, and tell her
what you think I meant.
Learn to cook, and remember how
we ate together, from the day she was born.
Keep the dog off the furniture
until he is old, an old friend of ours,
when it will be time
for you to dress carefully, prepare a speech,
write a letter and leave it unfinished
on our bed – and this daughter,
this face, this book,
you will commend to the future,
finished, beautiful, striding away.

Tell Laura I Love Her

My father (dead) reaches for the hand
of my mother (now young) and my sister
(long gone) clasps my mother's other hand.

They step together toward the sea.
They're chattering like gods.
How happy they are, my sister

suddenly gathered up
into my mother's arms,
kissed like a diamond.

It's time for me to turn for home
when a voice, a man's voice, says
You can join them if you want

and I'm running toward the sea,
my feet pressing into the sand,
brimming with oxygen and blood.

I want to get there, I want to
though my daughter sleeps
and my husband waits

who wouldn't want to
when their father returns
and their mother is young –

is this how it feels
to be forgiven? See –
the immaculate sunset

and their open arms
mouthing for me like a song
that was a hit before I was born.

I Thought It Was in Scotland

A FALKLANDS MEMOIR

Landing

Just to make things more frustrating
they show us porno films all night.

Rapiers are breaking up in the hold.
No news in case it puts us off.

In April, it's the height of winter.
When we land the sea is bright blue.

I thought it was in Scotland.
I thought it would be like *Platoon*.

The planes roar in & and drop & turn.
The beach blows up before my eyes

and the thought crosses my mind –
I was going to take Stacey to meet

my parents, but I never did.
And I never slept with her either.

I said goodbye from a phone box.
Couldn't wait for the pips to cut me off.

Not a Crap Hat

Now maybe I've been tabbing
for fifteen hours or more

and every step is stabbing
and every breath's a chore

and the point of rendezvous
of Operation Lucky Bastard

is in snow that can't been seen through
that's coming fucking faster –

and though these things are true
and I don't want to die here

this is what the Paras do
and I'm on the winning side here

and I wear my red beret
and I wear my Para wings

and you bet that come what may
I'm the master of these things.

May Your God Go with You

It's not what you expect
your sergeant to say

straight after *we expect*
to overpower the enemy

in two hours or less.
Eyebrows go up.

What the fuck was that?
He just finished saying

helicopters are on hand
to airlift the injured.

The injured will be back
on ship in twenty minutes.

We're on the starting line
like the fucking Grand National.

I was all right till he said that.
I was all right till he said that.

Wild Horses

They were sleeping in their trenches.
I could hear the bastards breathing

but back we crept, to make a plan
(discipline makes the Paras win).

Then we saw them
shifting in the mist.

There was nowhere to escape to
and no time to escape

so we threw ourselves down
and pressed our lips to the mud

and we knew we were dead men
as the hot stench of them

roared over us. We shook
beneath a screaming sky of hide

and waited without breathing
for death that didn't come.

Horses, someone whispered,
will not tread upon the living.

I saw it on the telly.
I saw it on the Grand National.

Dear Mum

A charge today, we beat them back!
~~It was Bigsy's 18th he died today~~

Am sick of Garibaldis & squeezy cheese!
~~I took out insurance like the sergeant said.~~

Cold here and more sheep than Wales
~~I have trench foot, I may lose some toes.~~

How is Dad how is the dog.
I'm in a hurry. We move off soon.

~~Mummy his brain~~
~~Came out on my hands~~

Serg says we'll be home by my birthday!
Funny that I can fight a war but I can't drink!

Hard to write cos it's very noisy!
~~Mummy I don't think you will know me.~~

~~I tried to hold his head together~~
~~I said it would be all right~~

I've been thinking how bad I used to be.
I'm sorry.

~~Tell Bigsy's mum~~
Your loving son.

Bruce Lee at Goose Green

We were outnumbered 3 to 1.
We didn't know it of course

until the Argie white flags
popped from the trenches

which was a long time away.
Before then a mine would snap

my arm at the root
& dump it twenty feet away.

I heard someone scream
I'm only 17 and the bastards

have blown off my arm
and I knew it was me.

The sky was long gone.
In its place was a pyrotechnic display.

My blood shone lovely
as the slow moving streams

of Cumbria where I grew up
& I knew Bruce Lee wouldn't give up.

He'd kill with one arm
twice as many as he did with two.

He'd find a way to get off a minefield –
by leaping, for instance. By leaping

as he did from the walls of my room
every morning of my life.

Fame!

I'm going to make it to heaven!
Light up the sky like a flame!

There was a lad from Wales
whose whole village turned out.

I shake hands with the Prince of Wales
and go to the pub straight after.

My mum and dad's mouths hang open
but why are they here who are they to me –

Jimmy and me both feel the same.
We sit in his bedroom drinking all day.

We can't stop laughing.
It's boiling and they're playing

all this crap music in the garden.
I don't really know where I am.

I'm going to live forever!
Baby remember my name!